"WHY DO PEOPLE DIE?"

Thanks to
Patrice Michelle Levin, M.A., and Rev. James J. Stewart

CITADEL PRESS BOOKS are published by

Kensington Publishing Corp.
850 Third Avenue
New York, NY 10022

All Kensington titles, imprints, and distributed lines are available at special
quantity discounts for bulk purchases for sales promotions, premiums,
fund-raising, educational, or institutional use. Special book excerpts or
customized printings can also be created to fit specific needs. For details,
write or phone the office of the Kensington special sales manager:
Kensington Publishing Corp., 850 Third Avenue, New York, NY 10022,
attn: Special Sales Department, phone 1-800-221-2647.

Citadel Press and the Citadel Logo are trademarks of Kensington Publishing
Corp.

First Kensington printing: July 2002

10 9 8 7 6 5 4 3 2 1

Printed in the United States of America

Cataloging data may be obtained from the Library of Congress.

ISBN 0-8184-0628-3

"WHY DO PEOPLE DIE?"

Helping your child understand
—with love and illustrations

CYNTHIA MacGREGOR
ILLUSTRATIONS BY DAVID CLARK

CITADEL PRESS
Kensington Publishing Corp.
www.kensingtonbooks.com

Do you remember the last pair of sneakers you had? You're not wearing them anymore, right? Why not?

Possibly you just outgrew them, but more likely you wore them out. Very few things last forever. Everything wears out eventually.

Sneakers wear out and get holes in the top or bottom. Toys wear out, till they're not good to play with anymore. Clothes tear, or wear thin, or their colors fade.

Sometimes something that's worn out—like jeans with holes in the knees—can be fixed. But eventually, things wear out badly enough that they can't be fixed.

People are like that, too. People are made up of parts that work to keep us going. Our hearts pump blood through our bodies, and other parts do other jobs.

Sometimes something can be fixed.

But when people—and animals, too—get very old, their bodies wear out. Some parts don't work very well. In time, some parts of the body stop working altogether.

Sometimes, too, a person's body, or a pet's body, is badly damaged in an accident. That's why it is very important to be careful crossing the street, so you don't get hit by a car or truck.

When a body wears out, either from old age or serious damage, a person or pet can die. Everyone dies, but fortunately most people don't die until they are very old.

What is dying?

When a person dies, he or she stops breathing and doesn't start again. He can't talk anymore, or see, or move. He can't kiss you. He can't hear you say, "I love you." He can't wave good-bye. His body has stopped working.

The same is true for a pet.

When a person or a pet dies, it's a sad time. You'll probably feel pretty bad. That's normal. You loved the person or the pet who died. You miss him.

Of course you feel sad and heavy inside. Maybe you feel like crying. That's okay, too.

It's okay to cry whether you're a girl or a boy. It's okay whether you're a little kid or a big kid or in-between. It's okay if you're a grownup, too. Grownups cry sometimes, too, you know.

You cry when you hurt. And when someone you care about dies, it hurts you inside yourself. So if your dog has died, or your funny Uncle Harry, who you always had such a good time with, has died…go ahead and let the tears come out. It's perfectly all right.

Grownups cry sometimes, too, you know.

When people die, there is usually a special religious service held in their honor, called a funeral. Sometimes when a pet dies, people have a funeral, too.

You may already have had a funeral for a goldfish or a turtle or other pet that died. Your parents may have put the turtle in a nice box. Then the family gathered together and talked about the turtle. Your mom or dad may have done most of the talking. Maybe your dad talked about how your turtle was a good pet, and friendly. He probably pointed out other nice things to say about the turtle.

Perhaps you talked about the turtle, too. You may have said how much you loved your pet. You may have spoken about how the turtle was good at keeping you company, how the turtle was fun to watch, and how much you're going to miss him now.

Other family members may have taken turns talking about him, too. You may have said a prayer together, or sung a song or hymn.

Your parents may have buried your turtle in the backyard, or the park, after the funeral. If they did, they probably buried him in the box they had put him in for the funeral.

Funerals for people are usually a lot like that, too.

Usually, but not always, the person who leads the funeral is a clergyperson, such as a minister, a rabbi, or a priest. This clergyperson will speak about the person who died, remembering all the nice things about him. We'll use Uncle Harry again as an example. We'll say it's Uncle Harry's funeral.

A clergyperson will speak about the person who died.

At many funerals, other people speak besides the clergyperson. Family members or friends may share the warm memories they have about Uncle Harry. They tell what he meant to them. They tell about how Uncle Harry was important in their lives.

What else happens at a funeral? The clergyperson may say some prayers, or lead everyone in praying together. There may be organ music or singing.

Just the way you may have buried your turtle after its funeral, people's bodies are usually buried after a funeral, too. Before and during the funeral, Uncle Harry's body will lie in a big, long, nice-looking wooden box called a coffin, or casket. (Both words mean the same thing.)

If Uncle Harry was a member of a special group, he might have a special kind of funeral or burial. For instance, if he was a soldier, he might have a flag draped over his coffin. Another soldier might play the bugle at the cemetery. It's a special way of honoring Uncle Harry.

Many of the people who went to the funeral will go to the cemetery for the burial.

All the cars that are driving to the cemetery get in line, one behind the other. They drive together slowly, almost like a parade. All the cars turn their lights on to show that they're all together. Traffic stops to let them pass.

The coffin with Uncle Harry's body in it rides in a special kind of car called a hearse. The hearse drives at the front of the line of cars. The line of cars, with the hearse at the front, is called a funeral procession.

After the funeral, the coffin, with the body inside, will be buried in the ground. But not in your backyard or the park! There is a special place, called a cemetery, for burying people who have died.

Friends and family will meet at home to remember Uncle Harry.

The family members and friends who went to the cemetery will probably go back to one family member's house and have something to eat together. They will continue talking about Uncle Harry, sharing good memories. Instead of concentrating on how sad they feel now, they may focus on remembering the good times they had with Uncle Harry while he was alive.

And everyone will take some time to comfort the people who are grieving—that is, those people who miss Uncle Harry. His closest family. His closest friends. The people he was special to—like you.

Some people even have a party when someone dies. That may seem odd to you. But getting over the loss of a close family member or friend isn't easy. Not even for a grownup. And everyone has a different way of dealing with the sadness.

Some people like to celebrate the life of the person who has died. They want to remember all the good things about that person and the happy times they had with that person. They prefer that to sitting around feeling sad because the person is gone.

It isn't that they don't miss Uncle Harry. They do! And at some time they will probably cry over him. But right now, they would rather look back on the happy times they shared with that person. They would rather remember all the nice things they especially liked about Uncle Harry. And they are happy that they got to enjoy being with him while he was alive.

People from different religions, or whose families originally come from different countries, have different traditions about what they do when someone dies. And some people celebrate. Even though they're sad at losing someone they loved, they're happy because they believe the person has gone on to a better life.

"Now, wait a minute!" you're probably thinking, "I thought a person who is dead has stopped living."

And you're right. But you see, different people have different ideas about what happens after a person dies.

Some people have different traditions when someone dies.

Some people believe that when a person dies, his or her spirit goes up to Heaven. Other people believe that a person's spirit goes into a new baby who is waiting to be born. Still other people believe other things. Your mom or dad can tell you what she or he believes.

Whatever your family believes about death, one thing is for sure. Only Uncle Harry's body is gone. But in a way, Uncle Harry will always be with you, inside you.

He will be with you in your memories. He will be with you in your thoughts. He will be with you whenever something reminds you of him. And nobody can ever take that away from you.

He will be inside you and inside all the other people who loved or cared about him while he was alive.

Did Uncle Harry always pat you on the shoulder and say, "How's the best kid in the world?" Every time someone pats you on the shoulder, or says you're a good kid, that will remind you of Uncle Harry.

Did Uncle Harry like to touch your nose, pretend he was ringing a doorbell, and say, "Ding-dong"? Every time someone touches your nose, or every time a doorbell rings "ding-dong," it will remind you of Uncle Harry.

At first you may get a sad feeling when this happens. It will remind you that Uncle Harry has died. But after a while, the sadness will start to wear off. Gradually you will hurt less. After a while, when someone says or does something that reminds you of Uncle Harry, you won't feel sad anymore. You'll just feel warm inside, remembering him, remembering all the good stuff you loved about him.

It's hard to believe that at first. It's hard to believe when you're missing Uncle Harry very badly. It's hard to believe when you keep thinking that you'll never get a piggyback ride from Uncle Harry again, you'll never see him pull a quarter out of your ear again, he'll never again call you "Short Stuff" and wink at you in that special way he had.

But gradually the hurt feelings will stop being so sharp. Gradually they'll calm down and fade and go away. Eventually you'll be left with only nice, warm memories of Uncle Harry— with just a little bit of sadness mixed in.

Uncle Harry's piggyback rides were always fun.

Sadness is what most people feel when anything—or anyone—they care about is taken away from them. One way to deal with that sadness is to cry. Another good way is to talk about it. Talk about how sad you feel. Talk about how much you loved Uncle Harry. Talk about how much you miss him. Talk about why.

When someone dies, it's a very emotional time. We all get lots of strong and sometimes jumbled feelings when someone dies. You may even feel angry.

If your mom sometimes takes a favorite toy away from you because it's time for dinner, you probably get angry at her. When someone you loves dies, you may feel angry too. Of course, nobody really took Uncle Harry away from you, but still you might feel angry about it.

Some kids even get angry at the person who died. Of course, Uncle Harry didn't <u>want</u> to die. Of course, he didn't do it in order to leave you. But you still might feel angry at Uncle Harry for leaving you, even though he didn't do it on purpose.

This isn't very logical. But it is understandable. Try to realize, though, that Uncle Harry didn't want to leave you. Death is a natural part of life, but still nobody wants to die and leave the people they love behind.

Another feeling you might have is loneliness.
This is a particular kind of sadness. It comes from
missing someone. You feel alone without that person.

But even though Uncle Harry has died, even though he's gone from your life, he isn't completely gone. Not as long as you remember him. Not as long as memories of him live on in your mind and your heart.

Uncle Harry will always be with you…in your thoughts, in your memory, in your heart…and nobody can ever take that away from you. So whether you believe that Uncle Harry is in Heaven, or being reborn as another person, or whether you don't believe the spirit goes anywhere special after death, Uncle Harry is in your heart and always will be. You can think about him and remember the fun times you had together, and the nice times, any time you want to.

The new baby reminds you of Uncle Harry.

You can help keep the memories of him alive inside you. One way is by talking to other people about him. Tell your friends about all the things he did that made him special. About all the things that made you love him. About all the things that made him Uncle Harry. Talk to your family, too. After all, they knew him, and they probably miss him about as much as you do.

Like we talked about earlier, even though Uncle Harry is dead, in a way he will always be alive inside you. He will be alive in your memories of him, in the things he did for you, in the things he taught you and showed you, and the things you say and do as a result of what he taught and showed you.

And he will be alive inside you in the love you still have for him. Love doesn't die just because the person does. Love can go on forever.

So if your Uncle Harry, or someone else you love, has died, give yourself a hug from that person by remembering how it felt to have his arms around you. If it was a pet who died, remember the tongue of your pet kissing you by licking his love to you, or how good you felt inside when you held your pet or looked at him.

People die. Pets die. But memories and love go on forever.